BECOMING AN ANIMAL DOCTOR

Exploring my dream goals

ADU ZOLA

ISBN: 9798371789341

DEDICATION

This book is dedicated to my Mum and Dad for believing in me and always supporting me. To my beautiful sister Kiki for her creativity and CAN DO attitude.

Also to my teachers and friends for their guidance and encouragment.

I LOVE YOU ALL

CONTENTS

CHAPTER ONE:

My Love for animals

I love animals. The reason I love animals is because those people that are lonely, animals help them not to feel lonely anymore. Those people have someone to love and take care of them. I started to love animals when I was eight. I saw an injured dog, the owner looked so worried and I wanted to make people happy by helping them with their favorite thing, their pet. That is why I love animals. I want them to make their future owners feel so happy. This is why I love animals.

CHAPTER TWO:

Spread the Love for animals

As earlier said, I want people to have someone to love and take care of. I want them not to be lonely anymore and those people whose pet is sick I will make sure t try my very best to make the animal better. I want animals to be happy and be healthy and have the energy to have fun and cuddle with their owners. Does it not feel good to have a healthy nice animal which you can love and which loves you back?

CHAPTER THREE:

Animals too can have fun

I want to help animals so that they can be able to help and play with their owners. Animals have many features that we don't know about and I want to be able to improve and help them with their amazing features. I want them to not die. We need animals in this world that is why vets are in the world to make sure animals are safe and cured so to release into the wild and be free.

CHAPTER FOUR:

Take care of the animals

I want to take care of animals. Animals need as much care as we humans need. As animals die, humans die as well, that is the rule of nature. So that is why we need veterinarians to be in the world. Veterinarians are the people who take care of animals. So if we do not take care of the animals, we are actually not taking care of ourselves. So we need to take care of animals.

CHAPTER FIVE:

Keep the animals healthy

I want animals to be in the best health condition as they ought to be. If they are healthy and well taken care of, humans would have the benefit of enjoying their company at all times without getting scared of catching any kind of diseases. Some kids like me would always say in their mind "I want to have a baby cat as a pet". When they get home, the kids would say please I want a cat, some parents will say yes but others might say no, because they fear catching illnesses. Taking care of any animal is a big responsibility. You have to take care of it with care and responsibility.

CHAPTER SIX:

Let's all live in peace

I want the world to have peace with animals. Some animals are dangerous like the lion, tiger, elephant, giraffe, cheater, gorilla and so on. With us vets in the world, we would be able to make peace with animals by: Teaching humans to stop killing animals for statures or for fun, it is wrong Educate humans to stop destroying the forests with fires, you are destroying their homes. Some snakes live in trees and other animals live in those forest. With no forest, these animals have no home.

CHAPTER SEVEN:

Learn more cool stuffs about animals

I want to understand more about animals. Animals have features we don't know about. Do you know that there is a type of snake that fly and there is a snake that swims and there are other features of animals that we don't know about? So, if you want to learn more about animals, you need to read books, watch YouTube videos and study. Learn more; look at animals not as monsters but as a friend. You don't know yet. You can study dogs, cats, snails, hamsters and other house pets you can have as your own. These will also help you to know how to take care of them.

CHAPTER EIGHT:

Create Drugs for the Animals

I want to learn how to make medicine for animals. We vets do not know every diseases that can be caused by animals so we Veterinarians need to look closer at animals to see if we can be able to make the animals feel well and up and doing. I want to learn how animals get the sicknesses they have and how to prevent them from happening again. We need to be more careful with our animals and make sure they do not get injured so as to save money for their food and living materials and to take care of ourselves too so we can all live together in peace and harmony.

Fun Facts About Some Animals

Did you know ???

1. The heart of a shrimp is located in its head.

2. A snail can sleep for three years.

3. The fingerprints of a koala are so indistinguishable from humans that they have on occasion been confused at a crime scene.

4. Slugs have four noses.

5. Elephants are the only animal that can't jump.

6. A rhinoceros' horn is made of hair.

7. It is possible to hypnotize a frog by placing it on its back and gently stroking its stomach.

8. It takes a sloth two weeks to digest its food.

9. Nearly three percent of the ice in Antarctic glaciers is penguin urine.

10. A cow gives nearly 200,000 glasses of milk in a lifetime.

11. Bats always turn left when leaving a cave.

12. Giraffes have no vocal chords.

13. Kangaroos can't fart.

14. An ostrich's eye is bigger than its brain.

15. Around 50 percent of orangutans have fractured bones, due to falling out of trees on a regular basis.

16. Frogs cannot vomit. If one absolutely has to, then it will vomit its entire stomach.

Culled from:
(https://www.thedodo.com/16-amazing-animal-facts-1094218100.html)

ABOUT THE AUTHOR

ADU ZOLA is a 10 years old girl aspiring to change the world in her own ways by caring for animals. She is a very compassionate and caring girl who loves to see everyone around her happy and well taken care of. She currently serves as an Office Help in her school . She enjoys playing chess and gardening. All creatures are dear to her.